Thoughts to
Remember

Thoughts to Remember

Nancy Moore Smith

To order additional copies of this book, contact:
Xlibris
844-714-8691
www.Xlibris.com
Orders@Xlibris.com
814875

Contents

About The Author

Born and Raised in the country before we had power
or a telephone. A lover of the out- of doors — flowers,
rocks and trees. God gifted me with a singing voice,
being a soloist for over 50 years. My English Teacher,
Caroline Turner, was my inspiration for writing.

Dedication

CAROLINE TURNER, MY ENGLISH TEACHER

AND

EDDIE ARNOLD SMITH, MY HUSBAND FOR HIS
PATIENCE AND HELP IN THIS ENDEAVOR

A Time

A time to remember
A Time to touch the hand of a friend
A Time to remember how we touched
　　each other's lives
A Time to feel warmth inside as our
　　minds go back
A Time to be still and absorb the
　　simple beauty around us
A Time to be quiet and think of the good
　　things that have come my way
A Time to lie down and rest body
　　and mind
A Time to realize tomorrow is a
　　brand new day.

Summer 2001

Another Year

Another year has gone by the way and
    tomorrow marks the beginning of a
    brand new day.

Another year is beginning with its
    mystery, promise, and hope; again you
    will search for the way and grope.

Another year to look ahead and time to
    reflect – there may be something better
    in store that you don't even suspect.

Another year, a month, even a day or
    two – bringing lots of good things
    to you.

December 30, 1981

Bethesda Cemetery

(Thoughts with Michael, my grandson of six)

A trip to the cemetery to walk
    among the stones –
You would think this is a lonely place,
    but they are not alone –
Mothers, Daddies, children, soldiers and
    all types of kin –
They are all part of a family from now
    until time shall end –
"Nana, did they go to heaven?"
"Nana, did they die?"
"Nana, how did they die?"
"Nana, will I go to heaven when I die?"
Michael thinks of Bethesda Cemetery as
    going to a part of heaven when he visits
    this place –
He walks and talks among the markers
    with a little child's wonder and grace –
"I love this place, Nana, I really do,
Can I come back here another day with you?"

May 1998

Bethesda Cemetery
Oak Trees

The sentinels are gone! No longer can they
    watch and hover
For over one hundred years they stood watch to
    protect the dead like a lover
Their limbs were spread wide and their
    roots grew deep
They had no thought of one day falling
    in a hep
They stood tall and strong like what they were,
    black oak trees
I never thought I would see the day they
    would be brought to their knees
Those who have long been asleep beneath their
    loving arms will miss them
They may shed a tear knowing their old friends
    are gone and may hum a hymn
There are those among us who loved them, and
    enjoyed the lichen on their bark and their dark green
leaves
We will remember them as a special creation
    of God - those stately old oak trees.

Sunday after church 2008

Black Gum Tree

Black gum, black gum, with your coat of red
    soon your leaves will fall and you will appear dead.
Your cloak is so brilliant with color in bright array
    In spring your leaves will return with the
    beginning of the day
I see your beauty in the middle of the pasture
    with sweet gum, with their multi-colored leaves
And then, – there you are with brilliant red leaves
    peeping out among the cedar trees
You seem unusually bright this year and,
    I wonder why?
I have no answer for that question.
    I would not even try!!
    Only God knows why.

Fall 2002
Driving through the country

Bobbie and Lewis

Bobbie and Lewis, that special pair
"Aunt" and "Uncle," with love to spare –
Dear friends to Mama and Daddy too –
And you know they both love you –
They would come to see us and spend a while –
I well remember this as a child –
They would come where we were
    and sit a spell –
Whether in the house or in the barn
    below the well.
1984

Communion Thoughts
at Bethesda

Thoughts again flood my mind and tears
    fill my eyes as I remember –
Thoughts of Daddy strong and tall giving
    his service to his fellow man and
    his God –
Thoughts of my family long gone, and
    recent gone from our sight to where
    They will always commune with God.

Communion Sunday in Church
January 14, 2009

Little Crepe Myrtle

One lowly crepe myrtle alone in the field
To persevere there takes a lot of zeal
There you stand in all your glory
I do not fully know your story
There among the cows and weeds
Along with pasture grass dropping seeds
Does the mother bird nest among your blooms?
Does she use this spot as her private room?
You give a splash of glowing color to an empty spot
Thriving and forging your way on this lowly plot
Folk passing by look your way and stare
They wonder how you manage to stay there
The aging house behind you where children used to play
Makes one wonder about a long-ago happy day
Little children used to play around on the ground
They watched and waved as people drove to town
I am glad you are there, you make me smile
Dear little crepe myrtle – so meek and mild.

August 19, 1997

For You

Birthdays are special days
    and yours is no exception –
Some are plain days and others
    bring a new direction –
A day of remembering a young
    lad who awaited his Special Day –
A day to reflect that you did
    things your way –
A day of remembering happy
    times past –
A day of looking forward to
    special future days –
Smiles to you on your Special Day
    and other Special Times –
Best wishes to you always in
    all that your life brings.

December 30, 1994

Cattle at Rest

The cattle are standing and lying in the woods
Where once young soldiers worked, rested and stood
To see the cattle like this was an unusual sight
    as I drove by
This scene took me by surprise; however, pleasing
    to the eye
My mind began to wonder to when I was a little child
Memories of young soldiers with jeeps, trucks and tanks
    on maneuvers there for a while
The cattle had no idea what the woods had sheltered within
They were just content to be there without any
    thought of what there once had been.

Summer 2006
Driving By

Dear Woods

Dear woods, I fear you are about to change –
You were once filled with troops and animals
        without any names
My, but the stories you could tell
Of young men, tanks and jeeps
Of tents, where they wrote and grabbed some sleep.

My mind goes back to when I was a child and
        I watched you all the while.
Of troops on maneuvers during World War II
They practiced in the fields, but returned in the
        evening for refuge with you
You covered them with your dense green leaves and
        they must have found comfort (solace) among the trees.

I have watched you and remembered all through the years
I have watched you grow and seen you change your cloak
I wonder about the stories you hold that no one
        ever wrote
I feel a lump in my throat and a certain sadness

But, to people and animal alike you have
        brought much gladness.

February 14, 1992

Fall Afternoon at Home

The sky is "Carolina blue" with
    clouds spread around like big fluffs of cotton
The fluffy clouds move ever so slowly
    as the sun comes shining through
The rays of the sun come down through
    the bare trees that have lost their leaves
Now I can see the big muscadine vines
    as they wind their way through the trees
Now I can see the rise and fall of the ground
    at the base of the sleeping trees
    I also see a few fallen trees and branches
    resting among the brown layers of leaves
I can also see a few green cedars
    dotting the scene and my magnolia too
The sky and clouds cover this scene, and
    the sun crowns all with long rays
    shining through
This is a time of rest for the woods
    waiting- for in a few months the
    spring will be
This somewhat bleak picture of winter's
    beauty was created by **Him,** for me to see.

November 26, 2011
9:00 AM
From my window

From the Window - Sunday Morning

From the window I see the mist
    The flowers, grass and trees are dew-kissed

The sun streams through with beams of light
    Bringing such beauty to all in sight

The haze is there – the droplets of dew
    Bringing bright sunshine today for you

The sun begins to brighten – what a bright light
    Coming down to the ground from that great height

The trees with their leaves in all different shapes
    Giving a feeling of peace down by the gate

The morning is still – the whole day is new
    God has given a brand new day to you.

July 26, 1992
8:20 AM

Glencairn Garden

To sit in this garden among the flowers and trees
The sound of the birds through the gentle blowing breeze
The shades of green of the new spring leaves
Give background for dogwood blossoms blowing in the breeze
The gentle rolling lawn with new grass so green
Moves down ever so slowly to the slow-flowing stream
The flowers blooming so bright in such profusion
Let you know this is not an illusion
The water from the fountain moves slowly to the lily pool
The sound is so peaceful and fills you with calm
You stroll along the path and think special thoughts
You sit on a bench and think of special times
You sit in the middle of this glorious outdoor room
You are surrounded by such beauty
    almost too much to consume.

April 20, 1993
In Glencairn Garden

Good Morning, Yard

I say good morning to my flowers –
And in return they smile and say good morning to you.
There is the smell of freshness after the nighttime rain –
Also, there are droplets of dew on the spider web –
    Like a daisy chain –
The green leaves on the trees have grown and
    come out as if overnight –
To my eyes and others' their shine is so bright –
I have a feeling of peace and joy as I see
    my flowers and trees grow –
All of this beauty came from God, and
    this I do know.

May 6, 2017
10:00 AM Saturday

I See You

I see You in the sunrise
I see You in the sky
I see You when the wind blows
I see You in the rain
I see You as a train goes by
I see You as a plane soars through the sky
I see You as snowflakes fly
I see You as I walk the fields
I see You in my mind's eye
I hold You most in my heart.

2000

My Garden

My garden is a place I love
so much a part of God's green earth
    A flower – blade of grass – even a
weed, each has its own special seed
    My thoughts, my wishes, my dreams
they all are here.
    All this beauty makes me know God
does care.
    The tiny lizard the tiny frog, my
lady bugs and the bugs in the log.
    All are a part of this abode
    I watch the flowers – I see them grow,
They know my thoughts – they told me so.
    This place brings me such joy
like a child with a new Christmas toy
    I can sit and dream and think special
Thoughts and thank God for all the beauty
He has wrought
    My garden – my very special place –
Thank you God for all Your grace.

Thanksgiving Day 1991
At Sherre's House

Kudzu

Kudzu covers, it grows and grows
    covers things like a new suit of clothes.
Trailers, bushes, and the stately tree
    if we stood still long enough it would cover
    even you and me.
In spring and summer it is green,
    in fall and winter yellow and brown.
If we don't keep moving, it would cover
    the town
It grows and covers by leaps and bounds,
    dropping from the trees and covering the ground
    all around.
Look at the shapes it forms, watch them grow
    there is a deer, a seahorse, even a crow.
Watch out! You have covered me! I can't see!
That's not a person, but a big bumble bee!
Kudzu has a little purple flower
    that smells so sweet
Like a juicy watermelon you would like to eat
It was brought here from Japan to cover our
    gullies and control erosion
    but alas, alas, I guess it is here to stay.
If you don't keep moving, it may cover you
    one day!

January 13, 1999

Listening

To listen to whatever I have to say
    not only once in a while, but any day
I may babble and go on and on
    you never seem to mind
You always appear to listen and give
    me undivided time
Even though your thoughts may be far
    away, you still give me time
Time to unwind and get it all out
    even if you do not understand what
    I am really talking about
To listen is being kind and understanding too
If someone did not take time to listen
    I do not know what I would do.

October 21, 1998

Little Crepe Myrtle Revisited

Little crepe myrtle, you continue to grow
In the spot where the farmer once did sow
How you continue to survive, I do not know
You look as if you have been attacked by a beehive
Your branches are straggly, some broken,
Yet they continue to grow
Buds still burst into crèpe-like blossoms;
How I do not know.
You are bright and you still glow - you are
A tough little bush – you told me so –
"I will survive the cows and the weeds,
If nothing more than the passerby to please."
You have been chewed on and broken
How do you survive?
By sheer willpower you keep alive,
Your blooms are still there,
They tell the story of God's love and glory.

August 2000

My Cedar Tree

(Beside Moore Road)

Dear cedar tree under which I have taken
    my rest
Of your shade you have given me
    your best
After years of giving to all your
    very best,
You appear to be slowly giving your
    fir a rest.
You have given joy and beauty to me when
    I was in your presence
I love your lovely blue berries and
    the birds do too
They have planted your children along
    our fence, to remember you
You are slipping away from living
    knowing you gave your best!
Part of you remains as part of my expansive
    yard
Your strong cedar log borders one of my
    garden paths
You now have a different life, as you age
    and moss appears
I saved this part of you, to be a part of
    my yard – for years.

June 5, 2011

My Daddy

A ruggedly handsome Clark Gable
look-alike was he
Tall, rawbone and strong like the
old oak tree
His olive skin was weathered and tan
At his funeral service, Reverend Roger
Melton said, "Rufus, was a man's man!"

Fall 2002

Thoughts

Daddy, eyes of blue
Cheek bones high and cheeks hollow
His stubborn black hair he combed
    straight back
His eyes were blue and steady and his
      Mustache trimmed just right.

2002

My Roots

My roots began in Bethesda Church as
    well as at home when I was a
    little child
My roots and faith grew and were nourished
    by those who loved and cared for me
    in my young life all the while
My roots are as deep as those of any
    tree and they keep me grounded as along
    my way I go
My roots are deep in God and His love for
    me – I know it is true –
    He told me so.

January 2008
In Bethesda Church during morning Service

Night Time Snow - Undisturbed Snow

The snow has fallen all through the night
 what a sight to be seen when it becomes
 first light
Everything is covered with fluffy white snow
The animals have found a place to bed down,
 even the buck and doe
Everything is quiet, there is a kind of peace
How wonderful it would be if all
 turmoil would cease
As I look out the window while all are asleep
Thoughts of this occasional beauty in
 my mind begin to creep
Now the snow is undisturbed as the
 night has been still
All that will change as someone tries
 to go up or down the hill
I will enjoy this moment of beauty
 as out the window I look
The calm and peaceful beauty of snow
 covering every crevice and nook
The picture of this special beauty will
 remain in my memory as back into
 the bed I leap
My thoughts will be pleasant ones as
 I cover up and go back to sleep
The snow has fallen all through the night.

January 2002
Before first light

Nine - Eleven

9 - 11

Our country grieves!
Our country mourns!
For those injured and unaccounted for,
For ourselves as we face the unknown.
Part of us died when the planes blasted
    the Trade Towers so high,
We could not comprehend this catastrophe
    causing so many to die.
Fire fighters and rescue workers came
    on the run,
They worked feverishly to save lives
    from sun to sun.
Many gave their all to save the
    loved ones of others
Now many grieve for them including
    families, fathers and mothers
God opened His loving arms to those
    Americans and others lost that day
God also opened His loving arms to us,
Who were fearful, prayful and wondering
    how this awful tragedy came our way.

September 11, 2001

Old House

Old house, you have seen love
you have seen joy
you have seen children
    with a Christmas toy
Old house, you have seen grief
you have seen pain
you have seen sunshine and rain
    But still you remain
Old house, you have survived strong wind
you have survived hailstorms
you have survived sleet and snow
    However, you are here for a reason
    and this you seem to know
Old house, your windows offer light
your windows offer breeze
your windows offer view
    of the world our eyes to please
Old house, we leave you with many
    memories to remember
We move to our new home
    and begin anew, but still we remember.

July 1980
The day we moved to our new home

Old School

Old school, we played in your yad
    we played on your porch
Old school, we played tag
    hopscotch and marbles too.

There was Red Rover, May I, Dodge Ball and
    Andy-over to name a few
There was baseball with a big stick
    for a bat.

Old school, you were there
    When first we learned our ABC's
Old school, it was there when
    we first heard about the "birds and bees."

You provided a place for learning
    for big kids and little ones alike
You provided us teachers that taught
    us about the Stars and Stripes

Old school, when we first entered your doors,
    we were so young and shy
Old school, when we became homesick and began to cry
    you understood why
We learned reading, 'riting and 'rithmetic
    some to the tune of "the hickory stick"
We learned spelling, history and
    geography too.

Unfinished -

Pain

There are times I want to *cry, cry, cry*
Sometimes in pain
Sometimes it has no name

To cry may help but then again, it only adds to the pain
The pain ripples, burns and stings and moves around
as if it has wings

I try to be brave – I try to be strong, but tears
of pain can not be all wrong
I try to only cry in secret – I try to be alone
and usually I cry when no one is home

Sometimes when I am feeling strong and everything
seems right
I want to cry again - is that so wrong?

Sometimes I cry – sometimes I sob,
but after that I turn it over to God.

December 20, 1991
Monday night, feeling weepy and in pain
After colon surgery

Playing in the Yard

(with Special Friends)

After a time of working in the yard, I wander
    to one of my outdoor rooms
As I sit upon the rustic bench I made from logs
    and a board
Here come my two "special friends" that follow my
    working steps ("Dudley" cat and "Buddy" dog)
They follow me around as I go about my creating
    and working
They are always excited when I say, "We are
    going out and play in the yard!"
This time to them and to me – this time of work -is
    great fun – even if it is long hours of the day.

April 2008

Poem of Thanks

Dear God, You gave me such a gift
    a wonderful gift to share
To sing my songs over hill and dale
    even most everywhere
To sing gives me peace and
    it gives me joy
A gift so special – my special gift
    you gave to me to share
You chose me, I know not why
    to lend this gift to me
To sing to the young, to sing for the old
    and those in-between
To sooth the crying child against my breast
    with a soft lullaby
Warms my heart with an inner peace
    and brings a tear to my eye
To watch little children listen so still
    listening to every word
Lets me know my message in song
    is surely being heard
To some the song may bring a tear
    to others memories of times gone by

Many places, many occasions
    each special in its own way
The joy of singing for my grandson's baptism
    and hushing his hardy cry
The joy of holding that same child in my arms
    after he ran down the aisle as I rehearsed wedding songs
As he watched me sing, with a special look,

and laid his little head on my shoulder and held on tight
To sing for the happy
    weddings full of joy
To sing for those who have gone to their reward
    in the sweet by and by
There have been many different occasions
    and many varied places, I have used this gift You gave
It is always an honor to sing in Your house,
    to Your people, with eager ears to hear
Thank you, God, for this gift You gave me
    this wonderful gift to share.

Summer 1992

Promised Snow

Alas, alas, the snow that was promised came
    while it was still daylight,
It fell quickly with dancing flakes flying
    around on into the night,
The countryside appears to have a calm and
    stillness as the flakes flurry by,
They are covering everything delicately as they
    come swirling from the sky,
When morning came – what a wondrous picture
    to behold,
Everything! Including trees and shrubs glisten
    like diamonds shiny and bold,
The snow is so delicate on the branches and
    vines,
Makes me remember each soft flake has their own
    special design,
I walk through my yard taking it all in
    and enjoying every spot,
There is also my special plant dropping in
    the big flower pot,
The time for the special snow is short as here
    comes the bright sun!
God has given us this special promised gift of
    beauty, as He fulfilled His promise by giving
    us His Son.

March 2, 2009

Some Thoughts in the 1990's (Four)

Wear a smile
Don't wear a frown
And spread sunshine all around.

A moment to remember
A moment to share
A moment to remember
I do care

Have good thoughts
Have a good day
Here is hoping
All good things come your way.

The days I remember are more than a few
The days I remember as good days with you.

The 1990's

Sounds of Childhood

The sounds of childhood are here no more
There are no little ones running in and out the door
No hand prints pressed upon the wall
Those that were little are now grown and tall
The sound of childish laughter is gone for a while
But when I remember it always makes me smile.

2001

Summer Scene

The light has moved from a small pocket to
    a widespread area of light with a beautiful glow
The straight trees and the crooked ones along with
    the shrub give a lovely scene they want to show
The swinging muscadine vines and the trailing ones too
    climb up the trees ever moving above
This glowing sight of sun and shades of green is a
    pleasing sight to share with those you love
This scene of beauty is in my woods as I look
    out my kitchen window
This is another scene for me to enjoy and smile
    Created by God, the Sender.

Summer 2011
Out my kitchen window

The Hand of Faith

I asked for a rock – a piece of stone
something for strength when I was forlorn

I asked for a rock – a piece of stone
when I was in pain and all alone

I asked for a rock – a piece of stone
to have and to hold, to be mine alone

I asked for a rock – a piece of stone
To hold in my hand to help weather the storm

My rock was there – strong like a stone
And gave me strength when I was forlorn

My rock was there – strong like a stone
To let me know I could bear the pain and not be alone

My rock was there – strong like a stone
To have strength to hold on and not be alone

My rock was there – strong like a stone
With that hand and others I weathered the storm.

October 17 and 18, 1993
Reflecting on my colon surgeries in 1991

The Love I Feel

I love all of you – there is love in my heart
Some I have come to love recently and
    others from the very start
There are different kinds of love as each of
    you know
There is love that is as "pure as the driven snow"
There is caring and kind love, love that is deep
    and grows and grows
Each of us gives and feels love in many different
    ways
There is the love of man and wife
There is the love of children, so close to
    our hearts
There is the love of family and extended kin
There is the love of dear friends who have stood by us
    extending a hand.

Spring 2003
Feeling low and blue

Sunday Evening

I am tired, somewhat weary
I heave a sigh and my eyes are somewhat blurry
I want to cry, I know not why.

The day has been good, the day has been full
The day was rainy and somewhat bleak
The fog rolled in across the creek.

The joy I felt as I returned to church
The welcome, the hugs, the expressions of love
The feeling that Someone had looked down from above.

The music, the songs, let me know I belong
Today has been full with family and friend
Tomorrow I will awaken and begin again.

February 23, 1992
9:45 PM
The first Sunday I went back to church after my second
surgery

Sunday Snow

The snow is falling outside the window,
   what a beautiful sight!
Covering all around with a blanket of white.
It comes from above, from a great height
Just think of what the flakes see as they
   continue their flight.
The flakes fly by as I look out the window,
I can not help but think of God, the Sender.
Though it is early day, they continue on
   their way
As they steadily fall, I wonder, how long
   will they stay.
How long will it last? I wonder, will the
   departure be soon and swift?
Dear Lord, thank You for this soft fluffy gift.
Memories flood through my mind, as I
   watch the falling snow,
Times of watching and participating in
   snows of long ago.
Thank You for the memories that we keep
   within
Thank You that we can recall them again
   and again.
The snow brightens the day and illuminates
   the night,
As it covers all around with this blanket
   of white.

November 19, 2000
In Bethesda Church as it snowed

Sounds of Time

Once again the mighty train goes through town,
    and I hear the lonesome whistle blow
This brings back memories of visiting with my Moore
    aunts in Rock Hill over fifty years ago
Now there is a new SOUND!! To be
    heard – night and day!!
A young man driving his small car – like a loud race car
    up and down the street – as he goes on his way
The car can be a LOUD!! six o'clock alarm,
    a call to brunch, lunch and a call for supper, too
I cannot forget his midnight ride like Paul Revere
    at one-thirty, three o'clock, six o'clock and neither
could you
I am here at Sherré and John's, recovering from surgery
    same as I had been exactly twenty-one years ago
Michael was a three-month-old baby – he helped me through
    that painful time with his cuddly little self, you know
There are memories of Sherré tenderly caring for me
    times of sheer joy – and yes – of real pain
There are recollections of good talks, some tears and
laughter too
    these were "making memory" times, and they will remain
It was on Thanksgiving Day twenty-one years ago – I wrote
    my poem "My Garden" and it calmed my nervous soul
These verses I am writing this morn after
Thanksgiving – are
    memories of the past and happenings of the present
Once again the train whistle blows – and the little car roars
on his way

This day – I will return to "my home" again, and begin memories of another day.

November 23, 2012
Written in Rock Hill, SC at John and Sherré's home

The Magnificent Seven

The "Magnificent Seven"
　　those amazing men
They were as close as any brothers
　　could have been
They met each other when they were young
They formed a strong bond that may seen
　　unusual to some
They went through school together and stayed
　　together through good and bad weather
Five of the boys grew up in town
Two of the boys in the country where fields
　　and cattle did abound
In high school they participated in clubs
　　and sports
With these activities they still had time
　　for studies and book reports
Their bond stayed close as college days
　　came and went
Some of them served their country and went
　　wherever they were sent
Their friendship continued strong when
　　they were grown
And had wives and families of their own

Their work took some of them to other states
　　and countries
They always kept in touch and remembered
　　times back home
When they retired they always found
　　time to be together

No matter if there was bad weather
These friends, along with their wives
    spent long weekends together
They would talk of days gone by, tell
    many stories and strengthen their bond
As about seventy years have gone by
    these "Magnificent" men still remember
    what once had been
They have lost three "brothers," namely
    Jimmy, Jimmy and Ben
The "Magnificent Seven" will be remembered
    as the strong "band of brothers" to
    the very end.

2017
Jimmy Barrett Jim Bell   Jimmy Doggette Framp Harper
Carter Martin Don Sadler Ben Smith

The View from My Window

The view from my window – what do I see
Green trees swaying like waves on the sea
Swaying slowly with stately grace
Each with its special shape – each having its place
The vines entwine throughout their lofty limbs
The designs they create were made by Him!
They greet me each morning and wave "Hello."

Even in the rain and also the snow
The rabbit and deer move below their cloak –
The bunny wiggles his nose, the deer sniffs the air
We know they are there – but they don't seem to care.

The clouds move around making their own shapes –
Rising and falling with their stately grace
At times moving slowly and again with great speed
Some like great puffs of cotton and others like
        a slender reed.

An airplane flies by with the greatest of ease –
There goes a flock of birds moving on
        like a blanket flapping in the breeze –
There may be a wasp or even a bee
Buzzing by for all to see.

After morning has passed with the dew
        and the mist

The bright noon day sun covers the
    view with a warm loving kiss –
Then the evening shadows and the setting sun
Let me know another day is done.

Spring 1998

Winter Snow

The snow is falling what beauty to see
As it gently falls around you and me.
Sometimes the flakes fall slow,
Soft like powder and then wet like dew-
As they gently fall around me and you.
Some flakes are so big, they look like
    a half-dollar,
When Mama saw snow, she would go outside
    and holler.
Each flake has their own special shape,
No two are alike as they fall by the lake.
Will the snow stick? I know not whether,
It all depends on how cold the weather.
It begins to cover the porch and even the tree,
As it gently falls around you and me.
The yard and the field take on an all
    new look,
It makes me think of winter scenes in a
    picture book.
Everything is covered – what a beautiful sight,
Covering everything with a blanket of white.

Winter 1999

The Walls of My Outdoor Room

The weather is cold as outside
    I walk
Picking up limbs and twigs to add to
    my wooden wall
I choose them and strip them for the
    right spot
I wonder what they would say of this lady
    if they could talk
This gives me pleasure as I make my search
    wondering where this special piece will work
I fit them together with love and affection
    moving them around in all directions
They have now found a home and can
    be together with "friends"
No longer are they scattered all around
    and without purpose
There is hard cedar, hickory, oak, and
    soft pine
They never thought they would be a
    part of my wall - it never entered their mind
I am getting cold – and I stand back and admire my work
Inside I go with a smile and pride,
    but I will return again wearing my cloak.

February 2009

Thoughts

In your life there is a
special love – one you can not explain

    One that remains in one's heart
through the wind and in the rain

    One that brings sunshine to the
gloom - one with a brightness that lights
up the room

    One that gives a warmth inside
and settles down to your very soul

    One that brings a smile a tender
thought and even a mist in your eyes

    One that holds many thoughts inside
and those that come out in the light of day

    One that has so many parts, one
can not explain

    In one's heart where this love lives – they will
always remain the same.

April 6, 1993

Thoughts in Glencairn Garden

I have come here to sit
I have come here to pray
I have come here to write letters
I have come here to hope for a better day
I have come here to think of those
    I love.

I have found calm here
I have found a certain peace
I have found memories here
I have found so much of God' beauty here
    wrapping around me like a piece of soft
    fluffy fleece.

April 20, 1993

Thoughts in Fall

You and me sitting under
a tree
I love you and you love
me
The breeze blowing
above our heads
With leaves in shades
of greens and reds.

Fall 1999

Beautiful Morning Scene

The long rays of sunshine coming through
    the trees
A heavy fog - like mist streaming down where
    there are no leaves
This unusual gray mist bunched together with
    the sun shining through
The sun is bright above – sending long beams
    to the ground – to find the dew
The sun has become brighter! The mist begins
    to fade!
What a beautiful, interesting sight our God
    has made.

March 21, 2008
8:50 AM
Looking out my kitchen window

Little Bird

Little bird, little bird, what is your song?
Looking from side to side to see that nothing
    is wrong
Holding a long piece of dry moss next to
    your breast
Perhaps you are looking for a special place
    to build your nest!
Now you are back! And the dry moss
    is gone!
And you still turn your head to and fro
    as you sing your song
Where are you building your nest?
    I would like to see!
Probably in a special place on the porch
    and one day – I may see.

March 7, 2008
8:00 AM
Looking out my kitchen window

For You

Birthdays are special days
    and yours is no exception –
Some are plain days and others
    bring a new direction –
A day of remembering a young
    lad who awaited his Special Day –
A day to reflect that you did
    things your way –
A day of remembering happy
    times past –
A day of looking forward to
    special future days –
Smiles to you on your Special Day
    and other special times –
Best wishes to you always in
    all that your life brings.

December 30, 1994

Glencairn Garden Visited

  I come here to be quiet and reflect
the cares of the day
  I come here to be quiet and absorb
the beauty all around
  The sounds and songs of the birds and
the water splashing in the pool
  The grass is green and the water
lilies white
  The flowers blooming by the walkway
with pink blossoms cheery and bright
  The squirrels scamper down
the path to the big oak tree
  Their thoughts are all centered on
play with no thought of me
  A robin hops by with breast
of red
  He looked my way and knew
there was nothing to dread
  The trees are almost still,
with a breeze ever so slight
  Before long they will fold their
branches and be ready for the night
  The paths and walkways are empty,
not a soul in sight
  There are memories everywhere
making the heart feel soft and bright
  My thoughts are many as I move
from bench to bench
  A butterfly flutters by and
maybe even a golden finch

As I sit and ponder my thoughts
a lady bug rushes by
I have no idea what she is
thinking, I would not even try
There is a peace here
amid the grass, water, flowers and trees
There are also thoughts of you
in the gentle blowing breeze
My cares seem somewhat lighter
as I go along my way
Tomorrow - I begin again
as I start a brand new day.

August 6, 2001
Written in Glencairn Garden
Rock Hill, South Carolina

Leaves of Fall

The leaves of fall are brilliant and bright
The all of a sudden they were gone –
    like overnight!
The beauty they have brought to us – makes
    us look in wonder and smile
We are so grateful these different colors and
    shapes have been with us for a brief while
The trees that have dropped their leaves, and
    are bare
They will rest for a while – preparing to give
    us new leaves – in spring to share.

Fall 2009

Thoughts in a Garden

To sit in a garden and think my thoughts
Listen to the birds as they sing and chirp
Watch them gather food for their young
Listen to the water gently fall
Watch the ripples move slowly in the pool
Look at the giant oaks with gnarled outstretched limbs
See the many shades of green that blend
Walk upon the grass as it flows around tree and shrub
See the flowers that have faded from their glory
See the new growth of leaves as it rushes to cover the old
blooms
Watch the squirrel scamper by to rush up the tree

My thoughts are many as they rush through my mind
Of sitting on a bench and remembering special times
Times of quiet and knowing someone is there
Someone to love, someone to care
Of times to be thankful for good things that have been
Times of sharing and times of dreaming
The thoughts of wonderment – how could this be
Knowing all too well, only God can create a tree.
Times of sitting alone and watching the blue sky
Remembering and knowing how thankful I am
Someone cares and loves me as I am.

April 28, 1994
Sitting in Glencairn Garden

'Tis a Day

'Tis a day to remember,
a day to have fun.

'Tis a day to tell you
that you are a special one.

'Tis a day to be happy,
a day to be free.

'Tis a day to stand tall,
like the old oak tree.

'Tis a day to give a smile
and to lose a frown.

'Tis a day to spread joy
to all those around.

'Tis a day to reflet
and to look ahead.

'Tis a day to be glad
And forget the sad.

'Tis a day to look ahead
to good things in store.

'Tis a day to look forward
to many, many more.

For Carolyn, Happy Birthday
January 26, 1982

Thoughts of Daddy

(Communion Sunday in church)

My thoughts go to Daddy, strong and good,
Tall and erect at the end of the pew –
Eyes straight ahead as he stood with the
    bread and then the wine – he passed
    to the people of God
On Communion Sundays my mind's eye
    sees him doing what he did so many years
I feel his presence, and think of times
    of years gone by
There is a lump in my throat and a
    tear in my eye as I remember.

January 7, 2007
Bethesda Presbyterian Church

Thoughts of Daddy
in Church

On this day of new beginnings
My thoughts wander to times past
To those gone before us from this Holy Place
I feel the presence of my Daddy
He walks up the aisle tall and erect
He has great dignity and pride
As he serves God and God's people
This raw-bone man of God and the earth
I indeed feel his presence in this Holy Place
And I see him in my mind's eye.

January 2012
Bethesda Presbyterian Church

York County Court House

I stand with pride and dignity and my
     colors moved with continuity
I was comfortable and easy on the eyes;
     for me this was no disguise.
My lines were smooth and warm with a blend
     that knew for what it all had been
My innermost chamber is fit for a queen,
     with hues of red and green; or was this
     just only a dream.

I stand with character upon this spot, and
     there are those who care a lot.
Part of me has become a shock – and I feel
     a little uneasy in my new frock.
The seams are crooked, the basting shows –
     I'm not sure I like my new clothes.
I am a Grand Lady that is tried and true-
     would you like this to happen to you?

October 12, 1977
Written after the court house repainting had begun

Coming Spring

Winter is waning, spring is peeping through
All this is possible because of You.

Flowers and trees with buds so light
Soon they will be bold and bright.

White, yellow and shades of green,
All this is very serene.

Pink, blue and lavender too,
All these colors for me and you.

March 14, 2000
Driving to work

Wild Hennett

(a beautiful weed)

The beautiful wild hennett is blooming
    with a peaceful lavender hue
Some fields, roadsides, yards, and other little
    spots are showing off their blossoms for
    me and you
I know it is a wild flower and you might
    say a weed
This year it has come to us in abundance
    from – I believe from long asleep seed
Everywhere I look in the countryside
    it is there!
It makes me feel good and gives me a smile
    soon the little flowers will fade and be back
    another year.

Spring 2020

You Are There

I see you as I walk around each
    flower and shrub
I see you in the springtime when I see
    the pink Easter bud (Red Bud)
You are there in my rustic outdoor
    rooms
They are a place of happiness, not a
    place of gloom
You are there when I walk my paths of
    brick and stepping stones
You are close by when I sit on a bench,
    when I am alone
There is the pond, gazebo, swing and even
    the bottle tree
All these things including the woods, birds
    and sounds of the day – make me think of THEE.

October 30, 2008
Walking in my yard

Your Day

This is to you on your special day;
May happiness and success always come your way.
Another milestone added to the journey of life –
Here is hoping everything will turn out right.

Hold up your head and give a smile
And keep that old confidence all the while.
This is YOUR DAY! Set apart from all the rest –
Use it to the fullest, knowing you have done
        your best.

December 30, 1980
Gene Ervin's Birthday

Another Year

Another year has gone by the way and
    tomorrow marks the beginning of a brand new day.

Another year is beginning with its
    mystery, promise and hope; again you
    will search for the way and grope.

Another year to look ahead and time to
    reflect – there may be something better
    in store that you don't even suspect.

Another year, a month, even a day or
    two – bringing lots of good things
    to you.

December 30, 1981

Michael Sadler

Michael Sadler, what a wonderful name
  From the top of your fine red head
  To the bottom of your little fat toes
  You bring such joy to us – goodness knows.

The night you were born you were such a delight
  To all of us there you were a beautiful sight.
  You arrived with a smile and a twinkle in your eye
  Your skin was so pretty and you did not even cry.

Your Momie was so happy and your Daddy so proud
  They both could have cried out loud
  Your "Nana" was there and Aunt Kim too
  Your "Poppie" was in the hall not knowing what to do
  We huddled around you and watched your every move.

We watched and watched you – what a delight
  We could have stayed and watched you all night
  You looked at us as if you knew
  We had waited a long time for you.

You became sick and gave us a scare
  But in your little heart you knew we were there
  The nurses tended you and gave you such care
  Momie and Daddy were always there.

You were a tough little fighter and strong as could be
  You said, "I'll show them – just wait and see."
  I'll show them what a fine boy I'll be
  We will have a good time together, one day, them and me.

You got well and came home soon
	Greeted by a welcome sign and blue balloons
	You came home in the middle of the night
	By the time you got there we looked a sight.

You were soft, cuddly, such a bundle of joy
	To all of us – you were like a new Christmas toy
	I held you – I rocked you – I sang little songs
	Enjoying every moment – knowing you would not be a
baby long.

So you see, Little Michael, my "little dooley bug"
	I love you so much and that comes with a hug
	I'm glad God sent you my way to kiss, hold and love.

P.S. When "Nana" gives kisses she always leaves her mark and
"Momie" always says "goodness me, we always know when
"Nana" has been here."

Written for Michael Sadler Walch's first birthday
July 23, 1992

Cousin Minnie

What a joy to know this little soul,
She seems so young - she will never grow old.

From the twinkle in her eye to the turn
        of her head,
You know from her there is nothing
        to dread.

Through years of toil and good times too
There is a beautiful spirit that comes
        shining through.

There is a saying tried and true
        "The joy you give others comes
        back to you."

She has a special way with words and
        brings to others a smile
Not only for a day, but for a long long
        while.

July 29, 1978
Cousin Minnie Bice

Uncle Perry

As a little girl sitting in a church pew,
I held your hand and gazed lovingly at you.
    You may not remember, but I surely do,
I thought there was no one quite like you.
    As a little girl listened as I sat
upon your knee, I gave a childish giggle
at the stories you told me.
    Once when I was sick, as sick as I
could be, I wanted you to play just one
more song for me.
    Your hands could move across the keys
like nothing I had seen, was this some
one playing, or only a dream?
    With you at the piano and Daddy on
the guitar, it seemed like heaven could not
be very far.
    The joy you bring to others with all
your musical notes, this is for real –
No joke.
    Continue to spread joy for those for
whom you play. I'm glad Perry Moore
passed my way.

November 5, 1977

SERGEANT ARMSTRONG

William, Bill, "Sarge", "Cotton-Top" or Friend –
    Most of us have never gone where this old soldier
    has been –

He Walks with pride and holds his head erect –
    You know by his appearance he can be very strict –

The cackle in his laugh and then the ready smile –
    Let you know he can be your friend all the while –

He takes command and follows the book and rule –
    When officers work under him, he doesn't like them
    "acting the fool"!

He believes when you are at work, - you work!
    That is not a time to play – He doesn't know about
    you – that's "HIS WAY"!

He has served York County, his community, and our
    grateful Nation –
    He is also one of God's special creations –

He cares for his family and his extended kin –
    He cares also for others and wants them to win –

Whether community leader, soldier, detention officer
   or the like –
   He believes if there is a job to be done, it is worth
   doing right –

William, Bill, "Sarge", "Cotton-Top" or Friend –
   We may not see the likes of him again –
   Call him, by his name, - but I call him, -"My Friend".

--Nany Moore Smith
August, 1997
For his retirement

Uncle Robert

A Special man was this one, given to
    us for a while;
A special man in so many ways, and he
    always wore a smile.
He delighted all the children, he
    brought joy to young and old,
His time he gave unselfishly, his heart
    was of purest gold.
He worked for peace and harmony at
    home and overseas.
He always tried to do his best, and I
    know his make was pleased.
He walked with pride and dignity, but
    not to proud to get down on his knees.
He was a tower of strength to others,
    and his gifts were from the heart;
He didn't want praise or glory, He
    just wanted to do his part.
He loved his family and all the folk
    that crossed his path each day,
Each of them benefitted from him
    having passed their way.
His eyes were blue as indigo his head
    shone like the sun; but to all of us
    who loved him---in the world there
    was only one-----.

Mon. night
10-31-77
By Nancy M. Smith

My Mother Margaret

My mother Margaret – what a wonderful one
    She cared for everyone under the sun.

She prayed for the good folk – and also the bad,
    She prayed for the "soldier boys" that were young lads.

She always had time for others – and her family alike
    She was known to go to someone's aid in the middle of
the night.

She gave of herself and it took its toll,
    Inside her body was a heart of gold.

She loved her husband – and her children too,
    But there was time, love and care for you and you.

She loved the elderly – the world's children you see,
    She had time for others and also for me.

She told us stories – she did special things,
    The sound of her voice still within me rings.

She helped us say our prayers and taught us psalms,
    She hugged me in the night and said to be calm.

She took us to pick blackberries when it was hot,
    She gave us a little scolding when we spilled our pot.
She sang songs with us in the pouring rain,
    While we stood under the trees down the cow-lane.
She huddled us around her like a mother hen,

Eugene cried so we vowed we'd not take him again.
She shared with others in need from our somewhat slim bounty,
She nursed and cared for the sick throughout this county.
She was there when they were born and gave a smile,
She was there when they died and went their last mile.
"She loved the world's people," as Daddy said,
"She was the best wife and companion," he said and said.
She had a forgiving heart and a beautiful soul,
God took her home to be with Him so she never grew old.
She loved beautiful things and simple things too,
She loved her flowers and the brown leaves too.
She had a special smile and had a special grace,
You knew there was love inside this face.
She gave me special things that live in my heart,
She seems so real at times as if we haven't been apart.

February 7, 1992 12:30 AM

Margaret Elizabeth Stephenson Moore
died September 1, 1960 at 52 years of age.

Communion Thoughts

Communion, a time of reflection and remembering -
The stillness of this sanctuary and the quiet –
The unusual quiet and stillness –
Memories of children watching the special service –
When I was a child we could not receive communion
     as we had not yet "joined the church"
Watching the adults eat the bread – broken crackers –
     representing Christ's broken body –
The sweet smell of the grape juice as it
     lingered in the air – how good it smelled
     to us children –
The same "fruit of the vine," representing
     Christ's blood shed for us –
And, of course, seeing my Daddy – tall and solemn -
Serving the elements as he has done
     so many years.

Sunday, October 3, 2004
Sitting during church in Bethesda Presbyterian Church

Daddy Serving Communion

Daddy, strong – standing erect, with hollow
   cheeks tanned from the sun, his blue
   eyes showing the seriousness of the task
   he is performing.
The hands of a farmer with fingers showing
   years of toil since childhood of working
   God's good earth.
Holding delicately, yet firmly, the plate of
   communion bread and later the communion
   grape juice to be served to the congregation
This he has done since a young man in
   his twenties
He has served God and this church in this
   special way
He may heave a deep sigh as he pauses at
   the end of each pew, but always erect and
   with great dignity
This man of the land, his family, his church,
   and of his God --- my Daddy.

April 6, 2003 Communion Sunday
During church – remembering at
Bethesda Presbyterian Church

To John

On Your Retirement

Your retirement day is here! Oh, golly-gee!
I bet you thought this day would never be.

You can rest awhile and do as your please,
And not have to look for your squad car keys.

Forget about uniforms with hats and ties,
And getting car mileage from forgetful guys.

Forget about confiscated cars and sales,
And delivering jury summons and hearing the wails.

I will remember the voice, the humor, the wit,
I wish you hadn't decided to call it quits.

Enjoy your farm, your cows and the gourds,
And most of all the great outdoors.

Enjoy the good times at home and away,
But don't forget to come to see us one day.

Remember the gals and remembers the guys,
This is no time for sad good-byes.

Remember the good times and forget the bad,
You may remember these as some of the best
times you ever had.

April 30, 1982
For Capt. John Boyd's Retirement

Little Michael

Little Michael Sadler – goodness knows
    I love you from the top of your red head
    to the tips of your little fat toes.

You are a "sugar lump;" – my cup of tea
    you give so much joy – goodness me!

You give a crinkled smile like a little flirt
    you make your Nana feel like "heaven on earth."

You wiggle your nose and you twist your head
    letting all of us know we have nothing to dread.

You lift your little arms and hold on tight-tight
    letting us know you really don't want to go "night-night."

You spread happiness wherever you go
    Giving big smiles and turning your head to and fro.

Your good disposition and beautiful skin
    I sure am glad we are kissing kin.

Your dark eyes - almost like pieces of coal
    make me feel good down to my very soul.

Without you, Little Michael, I don't know what we
    would do –
I am so glad God chose to send us you.

July 25, 1992
Written for Michael's first birthday, July 23, 1992

To Sherre'

To my little girl – my bright pearl,
    You bring joy to many in this world.

You give a smile – a friendly "hello,"
    You let them know you care – as on your way you go.

When I first saw you – my heart jumped for joy
    I was as happy as a child with a new toy.

I said, "She is so pretty," but goodness me –
    Now many say you look just like me.

Daddy was so excited he could not be still
    He was running around like someone on a tread mill.

He called our friends and our family too,
    Grandmama and Granddaddy - and they knew they
would love you.

Granddaddy Rufus was so excited – he said, "I'm so happy
    I could hop all the way to the barn! Mercy me!"

When I could hold you – I held you so tight,
    I didn't want to let you go, so we could go good-night.

I counted your fingers – I counted your toes,
    I kissed your cheeks and even your nose.

We had special time together – just you and me,
  I sang, I talked to you, cuddled you and you just looked
  at me.

I held you to my breast – and again held you tight
  We were in our own little world there, in the night.

We took you home, Daddy and I
  While the hospital folk waved good-bye.

I had dressed you so pretty – in a beautiful day-gown,
  We were all smiles – no frown to be found.

We arrived at home and to your new room,
  "Pinkie" was there and Grandmama came soon.

You were our baby girl - our bundle of joy,
  Our little girl with her Christmas toy.

Now you are grown – with your own little child
  Always know - Mama and Daddy love you, all the while.

Nancy Moore Smith
"Your Mama"
Written February 6, 1993 for your birthday tomorrow.

Judge Johnson

He charges to the jail with his robe just a-flying – "Somebody's mama is in my office,
> Just a cry'n."

"Gloria, #8 or #10 – Ah, hell, just let me in" – stopping in mid-stride to catch his breath –

"Guess I'll set his bond – what the heck – more damn people, Nancy, - I declare, I just oughta
> let 'em all out of here."

To Booking he goes to attend to the chore, charges back to his office to be met by some more.

Back to the jail he comes for a bond hearing amid all the commotion – he may give a "P/R" – or
> a "summons" if he takes a lawful notion.

He signs all the papers with the stroke of his pen – bolts out the door, only to come back again.

He listens with patience and writes a little note – Thank you for coming and rushes off to court.

He sits on his bench listening to cases – wondering how there could be so many disgraces.

He listens – comments – "Is that right?" – "Well, I'll declare" – "What in the world were you
> even doing there?"

He may give a scolding – pass sentence and say – "I don't want to see you in this court
> another day!"

The case is strange – the evidence perturbing. If you think this one is difficult – the last
> one was disturbing.

He keeps his cool and weighs all the facts – delivers his verdict with the greatest of tact.

The sheriff's officers frustrate him – it is no doubt – "Heck, they tell 'em to come see me

before they know what it's all about."
He issues their warrants and signs their tickets, you see, so many tickets for DUI – Glory be!
Sometimes they stretch his patience and cause him to fuss – There are times he wishes sheriff's

deputies and highway patrol officers would "just take a bus."
He always has a ready smile and a cheerful "Hello" – we sure as heck hate to see him go.
He has time for the "big people" and time for the "small" – He knows we are all God's creatures – after all.
At the end of the day, when everything is clear – He lights his cigar, takes the mail, and gets the

heck out of here.
He has made us smile, and given us such laughter – I know there is a special place for

Judge C. A. Johnson in the great Hereafter.

June 30, 1994

"Chief Of Chiefs"

A tower of a man once came this way
Even though when he came, he knew not how long
    he would stay.
Sometimes the road was not easy, and sometimes
    very hard,
But the road continued upward as long the way
    he did trod.
He was young and eager and ready to go,
He did not back down and he would tell you so-
His supervisor saw his potential and gave him
    a break,
Under his supervision some did shiver and quake.
He worked very hard and was steady, - but firm,
He let new officers and clerks know they had
    plenty to learn.
As time passed, he mellowed, but stayed on a roll,
But there was no doubt – he was in control.
No task was to great and neither to small,
Because, guess what? — he could do them all.
He could give a scolding and you would want to die,
One thing for sure, do not ever tell him a lie!
He worked very hard to better the Sheriff's
    Department and Detention Center, you see,
He wanted things to be better for you and for me.
He ran for the Office of Sheriff once, but that
    was not to be,
His loss of that position was the county's and
    law-enforcement's loss as we would see.
His time away from the department was filled with
    other leadership endeavors,

And then he came back to us – pushing and pulling
    levers.
He picked up where he left off and continued
    to work-
All who knew him, knew he was—no jerk!
He pulled us back together and began re-writing
    policies, you see-
Once again, he was looking after you and me.
Whether road officer, corporal, lieutenant,
    captain, chief deputy or serving as his own
    clerk,
He forged ahead and was not afraid of work.
There was a new jail to plan and build, to
    give over-crowding some relief,
Guess what? —he became the Detention Centers
    first Chief.
This was his new project, "his baby", you see,
He wanted everything good, right, and in order—
    the best they could be.
The task was great and tiring, and there were
    officials who needed a nudge,
But when he knew what he needed and what was the
    best for his officers, well-being, — he would,
    not budge.
There were times he was discouraged, and
    wanted to quit,
But then he would calm down and decide it was
    of no benefit.
Sometimes the officers did not understand him-
    this-tall man of steel,
Then there were times they really knew his
    heart was real.
He tended to keep his distance and may appear
    aloof,
But having worked with him so long, I knew

the truth.
"They do not have to like me, —but I want
them to respect the job I hold".
Most never realized that he had a heart of
gold.
Some might think by his sometime, stern manner,
him to be "bad"-
He would turn to me and say, "Nancy, they don't
know it, but I'm the best friend they ever had".
There was nothing he would not do if there was a
need,
From filing, moving, re-arranging, cooking, the
list goes on to—even pulling weeds.
He gave and he gave, —he gave us his best,
There is none among us who could pass that test!
He was caring and forgiving, and knew what to say,
But for fear his soft heart would show, -he kept
them as bay.
When time came to retire, —he worked for the
department to the very end-
I know this department and law-enforcement will
not see the likes of him again.

Nancy Moore Smith
November 2000

Holiday Thoughts

The joy of the season flows
    through our lives –
The anticipation and wonderment
    of the season –
The time of remembering and
    reflecting –
The joy of children with eyes
    full of wonder –
The smell of greenery around
    us –
The sounds of the season
    filling the air –
The feeling of love and caring
    for others –
The knowing we are also loved –
The quiet times for memories
    and reflection –
The knowledge that we were
    created in God's image –
The joy of the season flows
    through our lives.

December 18, 1990

Christmas

Christmas with all the rush and bustling
    around makes the mind slip into thoughts
    of days and times of long ago and not so
    long ago of persons, places and times gone by –
Christmas brings a lump in the throat and
    a mist to the eyes when we think of
    joyous times past, with those we love
    no longer present with us and those who
    are still among us –
Christmas gives an unusual warmth and
    caring for those around us and for the
    great love of God who sent His Son to us
    as a tiny babe to be our Savior –
Christmas thoughts some time overwhelm us
    and we hope all can be good and peaceful
    for those around the world –
Christmas brings a joyous feeling of
    sharing and caring, being with those we
    love and making new memories, remembering
    it is more blessed to give than receive –
Christmas is the smile and innocence of a
    little child as he tells you of Santa
    and the Baby Jesus' birthday and hold his
    little hands so filled with glee and reassurance.

December 25, 1993

Christmas Tide

Christmas is a time of joy
The smile of a child as he wishes for a toy.
A time of preparation of the home and of
    the heart
A time to keep in mind why it got its start.

Long ago in a far-away land
A tiny babe reached out His hand,
He touched shepherds, wise men and a little
    gray lamb –
His birth let us know God's love was spread
    throughout the land.

Let us remember Christmases of the past –
Memories of family times together and smiles
    of children that last.
Cedar, holly, pine and even mistletoe –
Candles, music boxes and choirs that make
    our hearts glow.

Christmas holds many memories for each of us –
Thoughts of times gone by –
Let the joy that comes to you at Christmas Tide,
Remain with you all the year through.

December 21, 1999
I wrote for the detention officers

Christmas Thoughts
in Bethesda Church

As I sit in this Holy Place – so many memories
    flood my mind – of times of old and of mankind –
Of Christmas times recent and long past –
Of times spent here, of message and song –
Of times as a little child when I stood beside
    a little manger –
Of the time I had to be tugged away from the
    manger that was so real to me –
Of fathers and sons dressed in bathrobes as they
    knelt as shepherds by the manger –
Of royally dressed men as the three kings bearing
    gifts for the Christ Child –
The little children in white and black vestments
    singing "Away in a Manger" with the little organ –
Of the cold outside, but the warmth inside from
    anticipation and joy –
Of Christmas candles flickering, making the magic
    of Christmas more inspiring –
Of the magic of Christmas filling us with joy –
Of memories, so real and close to the soul –
Of family and friends gone from our sight to where
    Christmas is always –
The simple beauty around me, of this church so close
    to my heart – as I sit in this Holy Place – so many memories
    flood my mind.

Sunday morning in Bethesda Presbyterian Church
December 13, 1998

Bethesda's Little Antique Organ

I am a small brown antique organ
that resides in beautiful historic
Bethesda Presbyterian Church.

The date above my keyboard reads 1876,
Philadelphia, Pennsylvania.

Goodness, my home is older than I am,
she was built in 1820.

No one today knows from whence I came,
but I have been a part of their lives
just the same.

I may have been the first musical
instrument here – no one knows for sure.

The "History of the Presbyterian Church
in South Carolina," under the pastorate of the
Reverend Benjamin P. Reid, between 1887 and
1893, states an organ was purchased – the first
musical instrument to be used at
Bethesda! That could have been me!!
The time frame fits!

I do know – generations of little
children have stood beside me and sang
their Sunday School songs.

I was even taken outside for Bible
School where children gathered around.

I was outside one summer for church
services when the sanctuary was being renovated.

They even took me out in the cemetery

on Easter mornings to see the sunrise for
God's people to sing.

I remember Sunday mornings when
Beginner and Primary little children stood
beside me and sang in the old Session room.

The children were, and still are, curious
about my size and my little keys and pedals.

Boys and even a "little girl" would press
a key while "Miss Nellie" played – she would
not miss a beat and only gave a
disapproving glance.

One "little girl" – especially loved to see
"Miss Nellie's" small fingers press my keys
and her small feet work my pedals.

I was retired after many years of
service – as there was no one to play me
and bring the music from my heart.

To my delight! Along came someone
who had loved me when she was a child.

She would come to the old Session Room
lift my lid – sit on my old worn stool and
play me for a while.

With great pride she would tell others
my story – sit down and play for them an
old tune.

Once again! I was remembered,
to my delight, she asked if I could
return to the sanctuary as part of
Christmas services as I had been long ago.

Her wish was granted – and my aged
heart swelled with joy, to know I would
again be a part of this church and her
people I had served.

I was placed beside the crimson tree,
with pride and with love she told my story.

The "little girl" - now grown – asked
those to stand who had sung with me when
they were little children.

They stood – old folk and those of other
ages – with big smiles, that would light
up the room – they remembered their
childhood with pride.

She played my shaky keys and
pumped my leaky bellows with the
pedals old and worn.

She also led everyone in singing
"Away in a Manger" as they had done
in years past.

One part I remember, and it makes
me swell with pride, is when each year –
The "little ones" sang "Away in a Manger"
during the annual Christmas pageant.

I now – again – can look forward to
Christmas – when I can again be a part
of God's children's memories – as I swell
with pride in my heart.

I am now back in the old Session
room, my home, with my memories –
I have a visitor, once in a while – the
"little girl" - now with hair of silver.

I am glad to see her – she seats
herself on my worn stool and plays a
little song.

I remember, and so does she,
sweet memories of special times we have
shared together.

December 20, 2011
A story of love and good memories

Thoughts of You

I Think of you at first light when The dew is on
   The ground
I Think of you as The sun begins to rise and spread
    glorious light all around\I think of you and remember you
    as I send my first prayers above
I Think of you and others as my prayers ascend
    on high like a dove
I Think of you as I move around doing my chores
    of the day
I Think of you as I walk the yard and remember,
    and again I pray
I Think of you as the day progresses while doing
    things that give me pleasure
I Think of you and wonder if your day is going smooth
    and hope you have success beyond measure
I Think of you as twilight comes and a mist begins
    to rise
I Think of you when the stars come out and the
    golden moon comes up and lights the darkened skies
I Think of you when I am ending
    my day
I Think of you as I lay down to sleep and
    then and there I hold you in my heart.

CPSIA information can be obtained
at www.ICGtesting.com
Printed in the USA
LVHW030032271122
733857LV00007B/663